PRIMARY SOURCES OF THE THIRTEEN COLONIES AND THE LOST COLONY ™

A Primary Source History of the Colony of
MARYLAND

LIZ SONNEBORN

rosen central
Primary Source™
The Rosen Publishing Group, Inc., New York

Published in 2006 by The Rosen Publishing Group, Inc.
29 East 21st Street, New York, NY 10010

Copyright © 2006 by The Rosen Publishing Group, Inc.

First Edition

Library of Congress Cataloging-in-Publication Data

Sonneborn, Liz.
A primary source history of the colony of Maryland/Liz Sonneborn.—1st ed.
    p. cm.—(Primary sources of the thirteen colonies and the Lost Colony)
Includes bibliographical references and index.
ISBN 1-4042-0427-X (lib. bdg.)
ISBN 1-4042-0672-8 (pbk. bdg.)
1. Maryland—History—Colonial period, ca. 1600-1775—Juvenile literature. 2. Maryland—History—1775-1865—Juvenile literature. 3. Maryland—History—Colonial period, ca. 1600-1775—Sources—Juvenile literature. 4. Maryland—History—1775-1865—Sources—Juvenile literature.
I. Title. II. Series.
F184.S68 2006
975.2'02—dc22

                                                              2004028881

Manufactured in the United States of America

On the cover: David Acheson Woodward painted *First Landing of Leonard Calvert in Maryland* around 1865 to 1870. The scene depicted by Woodward shows Governor Calvert, who extends his hand to the Native Americans, and Father Andrew White, who holds a cross, arriving in Maryland. The *Ark* and two rowboats can be seen in the background.

CONTENTS

INTRODUCTION

O n November 22, 1633, two small ships sailed from England. Onboard were about 150 people. Most of the passengers were men, but there may have been a few women and children as well. All were leaving their homes and heading off to a strange land. It would be the greatest adventure of their lives.

The larger of the two ships was the *Ark*. One of its passengers was Father Andrew White, a Jesuit priest. He later wrote a letter about the voyage that was widely published in England. White explained that the *Ark* traveled slowly. The crew did not want to lose sight of the smaller ship, the *Dove*.

The *Ark* and the *Dove*

But within only a few days, harsh winds blew up. Watching from the deck, White saw the ocean waters engulf the tiny *Dove*. As he wrote, "[I]ndeed we thought it was all over with her, and that she had been swallowed up in the deep whirlpools; for in a moment she had passed out of sight."

The *Ark* herself was soon caught in a storm. The mainsail was ripped in two. Those aboard prayed for God to save them, as they floated helplessly, unable to guide the ship's course until the water calmed.

Foul weather was only one of the trials the passengers faced. They lived in fear of meeting up with another ship full of thieving pirates or hostile sailors from a rival country. They also had to deal with crowded quarters, bland meals of salted meat and biscuits, and the crushing boredom of months at sea. According to White, they tried to break the tedium on

The *Ark* and *Dove* carried approximately 150 people during the four-month voyage from England to St. Clement's Island. The *Ark* was made of oak and iron, and measured about 120 feet (37 meters) long and 30 feet (9 m) wide. The *Dove*, a pinnace, or light sailing ship, measured about 50 feet (15 m) long and 15 feet (5 m) wide.

Christmas by celebrating with a little wine. "[T]hose who drank of it too freely," he wrote, "were seized the next day with a fever." Twelve of the sick passengers died.

Finally on January 3, 1634, the *Ark* reached Barbados, an island in the Caribbean Sea. The passengers disembarked, grateful to once again set foot on land. Three weeks later, the *Dove* arrived at the island. The *Ark*'s passengers cheered when they saw that the little ship had not been lost at sea after all.

From Barbados, the ships headed north, following the coast of the Atlantic Ocean. In early March, they entered a large body of water, the Chesapeake Bay. The ships then sailed up the Potomac River until they reached what White called "the wished-for country." They dropped anchor on the shore of an island they named St. Clement's.

On St. Clement's Island, the travelers erected a cross they made out of a tree trunk. White performed Mass, thanking God for their safe and successful journey. The day was March 25, known to Christians as Annunciation Day, a time for commemorating the archangel Gabriel's message to Mary that she would give birth to the Christ child. Appropriately, it was also New Year's Day in the old Julian calendar, which was then used by the English. On this New Year's Day, these immigrants found themselves beginning a new life in a new land.

White wrote that St. Clement's was covered with berry bushes and trees. But despite its fertile soil, the island was too small for a settlement. The settlers decided to sail to the mouth of the Potomac. About a mile (about 1.6 kilometers) from the shore, they began to build houses and clear fields. They called their settlement St. Mary's City. From these humble beginnings emerged Maryland, one of the original thirteen colonies in America.

CHAPTER 1

Years before the landing of the *Ark* and the *Dove*, one man had imagined a colony along the Chesapeake. He was George Calvert, a trusted adviser to England's king, James I (1566–1625). In recognition of Calvert's loyal service, James knighted him and gave him a generous annual pension. In 1621, the king also gave his adviser more than 2,300 acres (931 hectares) of rich land in Ireland. Calvert's home there was called the Manor of Baltimore. Calvert himself became known as the first Lord Baltimore. For generations, this title would be passed on to the heirs of the Calvert fortune.

Beginnings

Four years later, Calvert converted to Catholicism. The choice effectively ended his career in government. Under James I, England was officially a Protestant nation. Its national religion was the Church of England, also known as the Anglican Church. The Church of England was established in the sixteenth century by King Henry VIII, after the Catholic Church refused to grant him a divorce. During the reign of his daughter, Elizabeth I, Catholic and Protestant factions in England continually battled one another for power. These tensions persisted after James took the throne. Understandably, during his rule, Catholics in England were regarded with suspicion. They were certainly not welcome in the king's inner circle.

Newfoundland

Once he withdrew from government service, Calvert turned his attention to a new venture: starting an English colony in North

John Alfred Vintner painted this portrait of George Calvert, the first Lord Baltimore, around 1881. George Calvert, who was born around 1579, had been knighted by King James I in 1617 and served as a secretary of state and in Parliament. After he publicly declared himself a Catholic in 1625, Calvert resigned from government, and King Charles I granted him Irish peerage as Lord Baltimore. Calvert bought lands in Newfoundland and visited the colony of Virginia. He petitioned the king for holdings on both sides of the Chesapeake Bay but died in England in 1632 before seeing the king's charter that granted him and his heirs the colony called Terra Maria, or Maryland.

America. Calvert had already dabbled in colony building. He had been an investor with the Virginia Company, which financed Jamestown. Founded in 1607, Jamestown was the first permanent English settlement in what is now the United States.

By the 1620s, Calvert began eyeing lands to the north of Virginia. He decided the island of Newfoundland in present-day Canada could sustain an English settlement. Although no longer an official adviser to James, Calvert remained friendly enough with the king to secure a royal land grant on Newfoundland's southeast coast. Twice, he traveled there with a small group of settlers. But Calvert's dream quickly faded: the area was far too cold for a profitable colony.

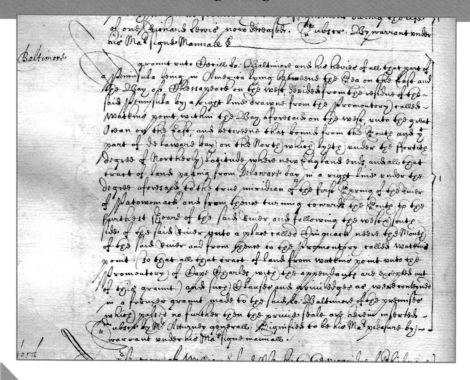

The Charter of Maryland, June 20, 1632, which Charles I granted to Lord Baltimore, includes language that refers to the boundaries of the original colony, such as the following: ". . . unto the true Meridian of the first Fountain of the River of Pattowmack [Potomac], thence verging toward the South, unto the further Bank of the said River, and following the same on the West and South, unto a certain place called Cinquack, situate near the Mouth of the said River . . ." For a partial transcription, see page 53.

Maria's Land

Calvert decided to try again, this time in a more hospitable climate. Appealing to James's successor, Charles I (who ruled from 1625 to 1649), Calvert sought a new grant north of Chesapeake Bay. At the time, this area was part of the royal colony of Virginia. Calvert was impressed by the region during a visit to Jamestown. The settlement's leaders, however, were not particularly happy to see Calvert. They were wary of him, both because he was a Catholic and because he clearly wanted to strip Virginia of some of its lands.

Calvert returned to England and continued to lobby for his land grant. His hard work finally paid off, though he did not live to see it. In June 1632, two months after Calvert's death, Charles I signed a charter granting a colony on the Chesapeake to the holder of the title Lord Baltimore. The original charter, written in Latin, called the colony *Terra Maria*, which was translated into English as Maryland. The name honored Charles's queen, Henrietta Maria.

The task of establishing the colony fell to the second Lord Baltimore—Calvert's eldest son, Cecilius. For months, he struggled to get financial backing for the colony. As a Catholic, he had trouble finding support. Investors in the Virginia Company made matters worse by spreading rumors about him. Finally, he found seventeen men, mostly Catholics, to fund the voyage and help establish the colony. They brought onboard more than 100 settlers, most of whom were Protestants.

Meeting Native Americans

After their long, arduous sea voyage, the Maryland colonists began building the settlement at St. Mary's. They were led by Cecilius Calvert's brother, Leonard, who was named governor of Maryland. Acting on Cecilius's instructions, one of his first priorities was meeting with the Native Americans in the region. Cecilius Calvert had learned a lesson from Jamestown's experiences with Native Americans. When they first arrived in Virginia, the Jamestown colonists had antagonized local Native Americans, especially the tribes of the powerful Powhatan confederacy. In 1622, the Powhatan tribes were angry enough to attack the English settlement and kill about 300 people.

A small group of Marylanders first paid a visit to the Piscataway to the north. Much to these Englishmen's relief, the Native Americans welcomed them. Another group led by Leonard Calvert

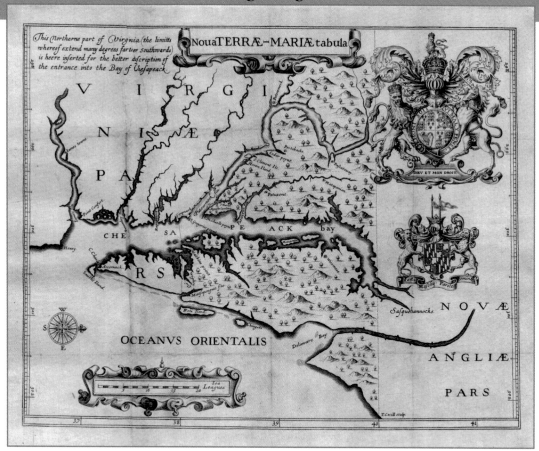

This map shows parts of Virginia and Maryland, and was printed in John Ogilby's atlas *America*, which was published in London in 1671. Ogilby based his map on engraver T. Cecill's map that appeared in William Peasley's promotional pamphlet, entitled *A Relation of Maryland* (1635). The map is usually referred to as Lord Baltimore's Map, and is the earliest map of Maryland and the first to include the coat of arms of Lord Baltimore.

approached the Yaocomaco tribe to the south. Calvert gave the Yaocomaco axes, hoes, and hatchets. He considered these English goods trade for the lands surrounding St. Mary's. The Native Americans, however, did not believe land could be bought or sold. They most likely received the goods as gifts of friendship.

The Marylanders were fairly lucky in their dealings with nearby Native Americans. Unlike the Powhatan of Virginia, the Native American groups in Maryland were not very powerful or

In 1590, Theodor de Bry engraved this print of the Native American village Secotan, which was located in North Carolina, and which was based on a 1585 watercolor by John White. The scene shows Native Americans doing various tasks and their fields of crops, which included tobacco *(top)*, maize with a border of pumpkins *(right)*, and sunflowers *(left)*. The Maryland colonists learned how to plant tobacco from the local Native Americans.

well organized. As a result, they were more inclined to make friends with the English than to fight them. In fact, these Native Americans embraced the English as potential allies. They particularly welcomed English promises to protect them from the belligerent Susquehannock to the north.

Building a Colony

Friendship with local Native American groups was crucial to the success of Maryland. From Native Americans, the colonists learned about the rich resources of their new home. For centuries, Native Americans in the region had been hunters and fishers. Game animals roamed across their lands, and the many rivers that poured into the Chesapeake were full of fish. Wild plants provided even more food.

Maryland Native Americans were also farmers. They taught the colonists to clear fields by girdling trees. Girdling involved killing a tree by cutting a ring of bark from its trunk. As its foliage disappeared, the earth below was exposed to sunlight, making it fit for planting.

Cecilius Calvert had told his colonists to plant corn as soon as they arrived. Again, his instructions were based on his knowledge of the Virginians' early mistakes in colony building. During their first winter, most of the original Jamestown settlers died because they had not bothered to grow their own food.

Another lesson from Virginia involved tobacco. Jamestown struggled to turn a profit until the Virginians began planting tobacco. Native Americans in the region grew a harsh tasting tobacco, which they smoked during religious rituals. The tobacco grown at Jamestown was a milder variety. It was exported to England, where men smoked it for pleasure.

Growing tobacco was hard work, but it paid huge benefits. Within five years, Maryland was producing 100,000 pounds (45,359 kilograms) of the tobacco leaves annually. The very success of Maryland became tied to the plant. Testifying to its importance, Hugh Jones, an Englishman in the colony, called tobacco "our meat, drinke, cloathing and monies."

CHAPTER 2

According to Maryland's charter, the Calvert family had complete control over the colony. Whoever held the title of Lord Baltimore was Maryland's proprietor. This meant that he owned all the land within Maryland's borders and could charge the colonists rent to use it. He was also allowed to tax the Marylanders and keep any money he collected. The only payment he owed to the king was two Native American arrows each year—a symbolic gesture showing the king's superiority without reducing the proprietor's income.

Troubling Times

The Maryland colony had gotten off to a fairly good start. But, for obvious reasons, Cecilius Calvert was determined to make his colony grow bigger and bigger. The more colonists living in Maryland, the more money he made. Calvert and his heirs stood to make an enormous fortune if he could persuade enough people to join in his venture.

Luring Settlers

To attract immigrants, Calvert offered to give land to colonists under certain conditions. They had to pay for their voyage and bring with them five able-bodied men between the ages of sixteen and fifty. In return, they received 2,000 acres (809 ha), which was reduced in 1635 to 1,000 acres (405 ha). These land grants were called manors. Settlers who brought fewer than five workers also could receive smaller grants.

Owners of manors could become quite wealthy. Furthermore, they were allowed to pass their land grants along to their heirs, ensuring that their family would prosper for years to come. Calvert demanded an annual fee from each manor owner.

Leonard Calvert was Cecilius Calvert's younger brother. The second Lord Baltimore made Leonard the first governor of the colony. When he arrived in Maryland, Leonard tried to govern with the help of two commissioners, but in February 1635, he called for the first assembly to meet. After various power struggles with the assembly, Governor Calvert agreed in 1638 to govern according to the laws of England, whereby the assembly had the right to initiate legislation.

Men who could not pay for their passage could become indentured servants. They agreed to work for a master for a set period of time, usually for four or five years. In exchange for their labor, the master paid for their transportation to Maryland and their food, lodging, and clothing during their period of service. Once their servitude ended, they were given a year's worth of corn and the right to farm 50 acres (20 ha).

Challenges to the Proprietor

As eager as he was to colonize Maryland, Calvert would have preferred that a few settlers leave. These people lived on Kent Island, the largest island in the Chesapeake Bay. Before the first Lord Baltimore received his charter, a Virginian named William Claiborne moved to the island. He built a church, a stockade, and a store and soon persuaded other settlers to join him.

Governor Leonard Calvert invited the Kent Islanders to become part of the Maryland colony. But Claiborne refused. He resented Calvert's interference in his affairs, insisting that

Maryland's charter did not apply to any lands already settled. After several violent clashes in 1635, the Calverts made peace with the Kent Islanders. Claiborne, however, was forced to flee his settlement, heading first to England, then back to Virginia.

In the colony's early years, the Marylanders also challenged Calvert's authority. By the charter, the proprietor could make all laws for Maryland, though he could ask advice from an assembly of colonists. From the beginning, the colonists were not pleased by the arrangement. They thought they should make the laws, with the proprietor acting as an informal adviser. After a few years of wrangling, they reached a compromise. The assembly began drafting laws, but it was careful to include a few guaranteed to make the proprietor happy. For instance, the assemblymen knew Calvert would appreciate their declaration that Claiborne, as an outlaw, should have all his property seized by the colony.

Civil War and Rebellion

In the early 1640s, England was engulfed in a political crisis. Its parliament included many Protestants who called themselves Puritans. They challenged the authority of Charles I, resulting in an all-out civil war. English Catholics and some Protestants remained loyal to the king, while most Puritans backed the opposition government led by Oliver Cromwell (1599–1658).

Cecilius Calvert wanted to keep the war out of Maryland politics. But his hopes were dashed by Richard Ingle, a Puritan merchant who sympathized with Cromwell's revolution. In 1644, Ingle arrived at St. Mary's, declaring "the king is no king." The Maryland authorities arrested Ingle for treason and sent him back to England. The next year, however, Ingle returned, bringing with him a small army.

The April 23, 1635, Battle of Pocomoke Sound is depicted in this hand-colored woodcut. Calvert's two vessels, *St. Helen* and *St. Margaret*, battled William Claiborne and the Kent Islanders' ship, the *Cockatrice*, at the mouth of the Pocomoke River. Claiborne was forced to surrender after the battle, which was the first naval battle in American history. Although a peace agreement with the Kent Islanders was reached and Claiborne soon fled from Maryland, Calvert would again encounter his adversary, who continued to work for Kent Island's exclusion from Maryland.

For their pay, Ingle told his men they could have anything they could steal. The army took over St. Mary's, entering the residences there and stripping them of anything of value. They even stole the glass from the windows. Seeing an opportunity in the chaos, William Claiborne returned to Kent Island and tried to take control over his old settlement. Finally in late 1646, Governor Leonard Calvert assembled his own army and restored order.

MARGARET BRENT: COLONIAL POLITICIAN

A member of a rich and powerful English family, Margaret Brent immigrated to Maryland with two brothers and a sister in 1638. Demanding large land grants from Governor Leonard Calvert, she became Maryland's first female landowner. When Calvert died in 1647, he left instructions that Brent should take charge of his affairs. The most pressing task was finding funds to pay the soldiers who defeated Richard Ingle's rebels in 1646. With the soldiers close to mutiny, she boldly sold Leonard Calvert's cattle to pay the men. When the proprietor Cecilius Calvert (Leonard's brother) criticized Brent's action, the Maryland assembly rallied around her, declaring "the Colony was safer in her hands than any man's in the Province."

Religious Struggles

To help restore peace among the colony's religious factions, the Maryland assembly passed An Act Concerning Religion in 1649. It formalized Maryland's policy of allowing Christians religious freedom. It promoted religious tolerance among Christians and even levied fines on anyone caught referring to another person's religion in an insulting way.

Further evidence of Maryland's commitment to Christian religious tolerance was Providence, a settlement at the mouth of the Severn River. It was founded by about 300 Puritans, who were persecuted in Virginia. They were invited to Maryland by William Stone, who became the colony's governor after Leonard Calvert's death.

Stone soon regretted his decision. In 1649, Cromwell's government beheaded Charles I. The news riled up the Severn settlers, who were uncomfortable living under the rule of a Catholic proprietor. Their leaders, with the help of William Claiborne, established a Puritan council to govern Maryland. Stone assembled an

This page *(left)* is from An Act Concerning Religion, which is also known as Maryland's Act of Toleration. Many scholars believe that Governor Leonard Calvert originally drafted the act in 1648, possibly with help from Father Andrew White. The law, which was approved by the assembly at St. Mary's City on April 21, 1649, set a policy of punishment and fines for intolerant behavior. It had no precedent elsewhere and tried to persuade Marylanders that the best policy in matters of religion was to keep their criticisms of other people's faith to themselves. The act established fines for people who openly denounced any belief, Christian or non-Christian. For a partial transcription of the act, see pages 53–54. Archaeologists discovered these rosary beads *(right)*, a string of beads used by Roman Catholics to count prayers, at an excavation site in St. Mary's City in 1979. Lord Baltimore had founded Maryland as a place where Catholics could worship openly and actively participate in the political affairs of the colony.

army to battle the rebels, but it was defeated by a Puritan force at the Battle of the Severn in 1654. After several more years, the two sides reached a peace agreement in which the Calvert family retained its power over the colony. The crisis ended, but, for Maryland, there were still plenty of troubled times ahead.

CHAPTER 3

I n the fifty years after Maryland's founding, the population of the colony grew quickly. In 1634, some 150 people arrived on the *Ark* and the *Dove*. In 1680, there were about 20,000 colonists in Maryland.

"Falling in Pieces"

The growing population, however, did not mean that the life of the average Marylander was getting much easier. Throughout the mid-seventeenth century, the colonists struggled with much more than political disputes. Day to day, they faced a battle against nature just to stay alive.

Death, Disease, and Hard Labor

The early Marylanders talked of "seasoning." This word referred to the time it took for settlers' bodies to adapt to their new environment. Part of seasoning was getting used to new foods. For instance, much of their diet consisted of corn, beans, and squash—all foods unknown to Europeans before their arrival in the Americas.

Far more difficult was coping with disease. Maryland's swamplands were a fertile breeding ground for mosquitoes. Because these insects often carried malaria, a single mosquito bite could end in death. Even more deadly than malaria were smallpox and influenza. Epidemics of these diseases ripped through Maryland's population, killing many and leaving the survivors weak and sickly. Largely because of disease, the life expectancy of Marylanders was low. In fact, about half of the number of children born in Maryland and Virginia during the seventeenth century, unlike the other colonies, died before their twentieth birthday.

George Alsop's 1666 map, entitled *A Land-Skip of the Province of Mary Land*, depicts animals, trees, Native Americans, houses, and a canoe in the Chesapeake area of Maryland. The map appeared in Alsop's *A Character of the Province of Maryland*, a promotional pamphlet that Alsop had published in London. The map uses names that were printed for the first time, such as Choptank, Wye, Chester, Sasafrix, Patapsco, Seauorne (Severn), and South rivers.

Another enemy to physical health was work. Growing tobacco was a backbreaking job. In the mid-seventeenth century, most new colonists were single men who worked as indentured servants. They were expected to work about fourteen hours each day, and if they were lazy, their masters had the right to beat them. The few women in Maryland also labored from sunrise to sunset, most often working on small farms with their husbands. These women spent their days grinding corn, milking cows, feeding chickens, maintaining small gardens, laundering clothes, and hauling water.

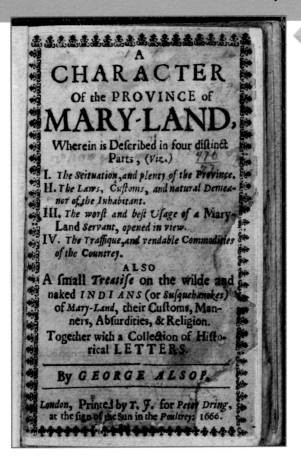

This is the title page of George Alsop's pamphlet *A Character of the Province of Maryland*, which Alsop had published by Peter Dring in London in 1666. In his promotional pamphlet, Alsop described his life as an indentured servant in the colony and how he became a successful farmer. Alsop's aim was to promote Maryland's promise as a growing and prosperous colony and to encourage others in England to settle in Maryland.

On the Rise

In 1666, with the backing of Cecilius Calvert, a planter named George Alsop published *A Character of the Province of Maryland*. As his pamphlet explained, Alsop himself had come to Maryland as an indentured servant before establishing his own farm. He wrote glowingly about a servant's life in Maryland and assured those considering indenturing themselves that, once they were freed, they were sure to "live passingly well."

Designed as publicity for the colony, Alsop's pamphlet certainly oversold the quality of life an indentured servant could expect. But its suggestion that servants could become successful planters had some truth to it. Some planters, like Alsop, made a decent living from the 50 acres (20 ha) they could claim as freemen. A few servants even became wealthy, owning farms of more than 1,000 acres (405 ha).

Some former servants held posts in the proprietor's government. They served as militia leaders and worked as justices and sheriffs. These jobs gave men from impoverished backgrounds not only a good income, but also a fair amount of power—but only as long as they stayed in the good graces of the proprietor.

Fighting the Proprietor

By the mid-seventeenth century, the Maryland assembly had two houses. The more elite upper house was made up of counselors chosen by the proprietor. The more democratic lower house was composed of elected representatives. These representatives were largely successful planters, including a few self-made men. Increasingly, the two houses came in conflict, as average Marylanders started questioning whether the proprietor was looking after their best interests.

Marylanders had plenty of complaints. One of their biggest gripes was that the proprietor was not doing enough to protect them from Native Americans. To some extent, the colonists were unrealistic about the Native American threat. In the decades after Maryland's founding, disease had essentially destroyed all nearby tribes. In 1652, even the once fearsome Susquehannock were so weak that they agreed to a peace treaty in which they gave up most of their land. The still powerful Seneca, however, were moving into the Susquehannock's former territory, renewing anxieties over Native American attacks.

Some of the proprietor's decisions about how the assembly should be run also earned the colonists' wrath. Within Maryland, only men with property could vote for their representatives. When the proprietor raised the amount of property needed, many Marylanders cried foul, insisting that he was trying to bolster the power of his wealthy friends. The proprietor also took a misstep by ruling that each county in the colony could send only two men to the assembly rather than four as they had in the past. Calvert maintained he just wanted to keep the size of the assembly manageable, but many colonists still objected.

Another grievance of many Anglican colonists was Maryland's policy of religious tolerance. It drew people from other colonies who were members of persecuted groups, such as the Quakers and the Presbyterians. The Anglicans, however, wanted the Church of England to be the colony's official religion. They were suspicious of people of other religions, particularly Catholics. Adding to their hostility was the fact that many of the proprietor's counselors were Catholic.

Protestants Revolt

With their growing discontent, Marylanders became more outspoken in their criticism. In 1675, a few wrote an angry petition, detailing the Calverts' abuses. Two of the petition's authors were hanged.

By 1681, a group of Protestants were in open revolt. They were led by Josias Fendall, a former governor of the colony, and John Coode, a member of the assembly. Fendall was eventually banished for plotting to imprison the third Lord Baltimore, Charles Calvert. According to the governor of Virginia, the colony was completely out of control: "Maryland is now in torment and not only troubled with our disease, poverty, but in very great danger of falling in pieces."

An Act for Erecting a County Court is one of the laws recorded in the proceedings and acts of the General Assembly of Maryland in 1638. Although the proprietors of Maryland increasingly clashed with the General Assembly over issues of political power and legislation, the laws that were enacted, including the establishment of a county court, helped to stabilize the colony. For a partial transcription of the act, see page 54.

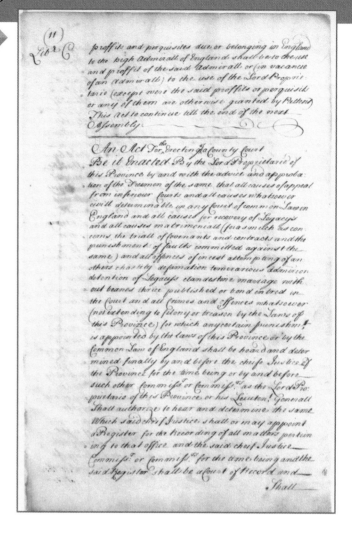

But rebelling colonists were not the proprietor's problem. While they were rising up, the English king Charles II (1630–1685) offered a proprietorship to William Penn, a Quaker leader. Penn's land grant, known as Pennsylvania, was just north of Maryland, but its boundaries were not exactly clear. Calvert feared Penn would take over lands Calvert felt belonged to Maryland. Calvert and Penn met twice in 1684 to resolve the matter but were unable to make any agreements. Desperate to preserve his land claims, Calvert sailed to England to make his case before royal officials. Embroiled in political battles there, he never returned to Maryland.

Judge George Jeffreys (1645–1689), was also known as the Hanging Judge for ordering the executions of about 200 people and the selling of hundreds of others into slavery in the American colonies. Jeffreys, James II's influential adviser and Lord Chancellor, worked to force the Church of England to accept the king's pro-Catholic policies. When William of Orange overthrew James II, Jeffreys tried to escape from England disguised as a sailor. He is depicted here being discovered and arrested at Wapping, England, during the Glorious Revolution in December 1688. Jeffreys died four months later in the Tower of London.

During Calvert's absence, the Catholic king James II (1633–1701) took the English throne. In 1688, William of Orange, with the help and authority of Parliament, challenged the king's rule. In what became known as the Glorious Revolution, William's army arrived in London and deposed James, making William and his wife, Mary, the new Protestant king and queen. Calvert wrote a letter to Maryland officials, telling them to accept these monarchs as England's rightful rulers. The letter, however, never arrived.

In the summer of 1689, as Marylanders learned about the revolution, Coode saw an opportunity. He rallied a group of successful planters to join his Protestant Association. Carrying arms, they marched to St. Mary's City. The authorities there had little choice but to surrender. Without a single shot being fired, the Calvert family lost its proprietorship. Maryland became a royal colony under the direct rule of the English crown.

CHAPTER 4

With King William's blessing, Maryland's assembly began to make some changes. It set about repealing some old laws, revising others, and making a few new ones of its own. But perhaps the most sweeping change came in 1692, with the passage of the Act for the Service of Almighty God and the Establishment of the Protestant Religion. This act made the Church of England the established church of colonial Maryland. Not only had the proprietorship ceased to exist, the proprietor's vision of religious freedom in Maryland was gone as well.

Changing Times

The assembly passed other laws to support the new official church. Marylanders were to respect the Sunday Sabbath. In order to serve in the assembly or testify in court, they had to pledge an oath of fidelity to the Protestant king. And to fund the construction of Anglican churches and pay the salaries of Anglican ministers, each taxpayer had to give the colony 40 pounds (18 kg) of tobacco every year.

Quakers and Catholics

Understandably, the many non-Anglicans in Maryland were upset. Some Puritans and Presbyterians resisted the new tax. They paid it reluctantly, offering only the worst quality of tobacco. Maryland's Quakers were even angrier. Some refused to pay the tax at all, even though they were threatened with stiff fines or even jail time. To the Quakers, the required oathtaking was even worse than the tax. Because they refused to take the oath, they were excluded from Maryland politics. They were also barred from testifying in court, placing them in a vulnerable position if they were charged with a crime or if they wanted to sue another colonist.

Long held in suspicion, Catholics also suffered under the new laws. They were forbidden from being baptized or holding Mass in public. Attempting to convert a Protestant to Catholicism became illegal. The Maryland government tried to discourage Catholics from Ireland from immigrating to the colony as well. A master had to pay a special fee if he took on an Irish Catholic as an indentured servant.

In 1715, the new English king, George I (1660–1727), returned the proprietorship of Maryland to the fourth Lord Baltimore, Benedict Leonard Calvert, who had converted to the Anglican Church. The non-Anglicans hoped the proprietor would restore religious freedom to the colony. But they were soon disappointed. Under the renewed proprietorship, they were still treated like second-class citizens.

The Tobacco Merchants

In the early eighteenth century, Maryland society was not just divided by religion. Increasingly, it was also divided by wealth. Some Marylanders became very successful. As their wealth grew, so did their power in the colony. But other Marylanders saw their opportunities shrink. As their prospects dimmed, so did their chance to build a decent life for themselves and their families.

Many of the newly wealthy were middlemen in the tobacco industry. After the harvest, small farmers took their tobacco to English ships, which transported the crop to England for sale. At first, farmers were not paid for their tobacco until it was sold. Having to wait months for payment was a hardship for these farmers, who needed to buy metal tools and other necessities to keep their farms going.

This print from 1697 shows the Charles County courthouse and ordinary (an eating house, or inn, that serves meals). The illustration also depicts the courthouse's clapboard siding, brick chimney, two-story porch, and casement windows (which were commonly used in the homes of wealthy colonists). A simpler, one-room building, such as that of the old house pictured here, was the typical home design for most colonists in Maryland.

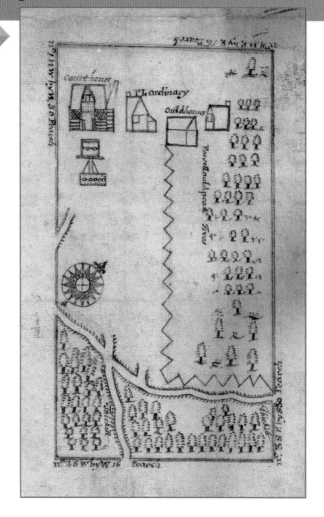

Some men saw an opportunity in the farmers' situation. They offered goods to small farmers in exchange for their tobacco and then sold the tobacco themselves for a profit. These tobacco merchants were generally successful planters or professionals (such as doctors or lawyers) with money to invest.

In the eighteenth century, the price of tobacco was constantly changing. When the price was high, these merchants made a great deal of money. Their profits were large enough that, even when the tobacco price fell, they still made a good living. In time, these merchant-planters began to control more and more of Maryland's wealth. Their children tended to marry children from other well-to-do families, keeping their riches in the hands of just a few.

Farmers and Servants

At the same time, small farmers found they had fewer chances to improve their lot. As tobacco prices were falling, land was becoming more expensive. (In the twenty years between 1680 and 1700, the price of land doubled.) Other costs of running a farm, such as buying tools and hiring farm hands, also remained high.

More so than in the early years of the colony, small farmers had to struggle to make a living. Former indentured servants were in an even worse situation. At one time, ex-servants could work to become landowners and sometimes even wealthy planters. But by the early eighteenth century, far fewer could ever hope to have farms of their own.

As opportunity for servants dwindled, fewer Englishmen were willing to come to Maryland. Those who were eager to come were likely to be unskilled and desperately poor. The supply of indentured servants dried up even more as several wars broke out in Europe, making travel across the Atlantic more difficult and dangerous. These conflicts also offered poor men the chance to work as mercenaries, or paid soldiers, a profession that paid much better than indentured servitude. As a result, the cost of indentured servants rose high enough that many farmers could no longer afford them.

A Slave Colony

Even wealthier farmers balked at the price of indentured servants. They began to rely more on another group of workers—black slaves from Africa. Slaves were more expensive than servants. But servants only worked for their masters for a set number of years. Slaves, on the other hand, were forced to give their masters a lifetime of labor. Even better for the masters, slaves' children became slaves as well.

This illustration is a detail, called a cartouche, from *A Map of the Most Inhabited Part of Virginia Containing the Whole Province of Maryland with Part of Pensilvania, New Jersey and North Carolina*, which was drawn by Joshua Fry and Peter Jefferson in 1775. The scene pictured is a common scene along the Chesapeake, showing a tobacco wharf, barrels of tobacco, merchants, and slaves involved in the transport of the tobacco to market. As a crop, tobacco required much manual labor to produce. Wealthy planters began to depend on the practice of slavery to supply their much-needed workforce.

In the early eighteenth century, slavery grew rapidly. The new wealthy class could afford to import slaves in large numbers. From 1695 to 1708 alone, 4,000 slaves arrived in the colony. These slaves took over much of the painstaking labor that made Maryland's tobacco industry possible.

When slaves first laid eyes on Maryland, most were weak and sick from the horrific sea voyage from Africa. Unlike white immigrants to the colony, they hardly saw their new home as a land of opportunity. In Maryland, they faced a world without promise and a future without hope.

CHAPTER 5

Prosperity

In early eighteenth-century Maryland, wealthy planters and struggling farmers had one thing in common: both suffered when tobacco prices fell. In Virginia, lawmakers tried to deal with the problem by establishing an inspection system for all Virginian tobacco. Only tobacco judged to be top quality could be shipped from Virginia to England. This way, Virginia lawmakers concluded, they could make sure that the price for their harvests stayed high.

After years of debate, Maryland finally passed its own tobacco inspection act in 1747. The law established eighty public warehouses, where farmers brought their tobacco to be inspected. Only high quality tobacco was deemed sellable. The rest was burned. By the time this system was in place, however, the colony's complete reliance on tobacco was coming to an end. Although Maryland still produced plenty of tobacco for export, other profitable industries began to grow. And with them, the economy of Maryland grew as well, drawing the colony into its golden age.

Wheat, Meat, and Ships

In the mid-1700s, trade ships from New England traveling south regularly visited the Chesapeake Bay. Maryland farmers discovered the traders aboard were eager to buy wheat. The New Englanders knew there was a market for Maryland wheat in the West Indies, where they could trade it for slaves, rum, and sugar. Often, on the return trip, their ships would again stop off in Maryland to purchase more wheat, which they transported to markets in the northern colonies of Massachusetts and Rhode Island.

The name of the artist of this work, entitled *Grey's Inn Creek Shipyard*, is not known today, but the painting was made around 1750. It depicts a variety of vessels that were commonly seen on Chesapeake Bay in the eighteenth century, including a log canoe, brig, sloop, tobacco ship, schooner, and shallop, which is a type of two-masted ship. With its location along the northern part of the Chesapeake, Maryland became vital to the shipbuilding industry, not only because of its ports but also because of its timber.

This trade in wheat was a boon to many Marylanders. In some areas in eastern Maryland, the land was too sandy to grow tobacco but it was just right for wheat. Even in areas where tobacco could be cultivated, farmers preferred growing wheat and corn. These crops did not require the constant tending that tobacco did. They also did not exhaust the nutrients in the soil nearly as quickly, so cleared fields could be used far longer.

Wheat farmers sometimes raised livestock as well. Herds of sheep, cattle, and hogs provided meat for Maryland farm families. And traders passing through were happy to buy any extras.

The rise in wheat exports helped create a new industry in Maryland—shipping. Marylanders had long built ships to navigate the bay and the many rivers that fed into it. But in the early eighteenth century, the colony's shipbuilders began producing bigger boats able to transport wheat and other goods. Over time, they experimented with ship designs, developing a reputation for well constructed, graceful vessels. Eventually, Maryland ship-builders were considered among the best in all America.

Town Life

When tobacco was Maryland's main export, trading centers were sprinkled throughout the colony's farming regions. In the summer, farmers gathered at these trading centers to sell their tobacco harvest. But they were largely empty the rest of the year.

When farmers began growing more grain, however, trading areas were active all year long. Corn was ready for sale in the spring, whereas wheat was harvested in the fall. Livestock and meat were traded in all seasons. With farmers always coming and going, tavern keepers and merchants set up shop at these trading centers. Wagon makers and craftspeople also settled there to sell their wares. In time, these centers became towns and even cities.

One bustling town was Baltimore. Founded in 1729, it included about twenty-five buildings and was the site of several annual fairs by 1750. Baltimore also became an important center of Maryland's growing iron industry. By the mid-eighteenth century, the town boasted six ironworks.

Settling the West

At the same time, Marylanders began flocking west. They were encouraged by the fifth Lord Baltimore, Charles Calvert. The proprietor was worried about a border dispute with Virginia. He wanted Marylanders to settle along the upper reaches of the Potomac River to keep Virginians from taking over the area.

Daniel Dulany, pictured here around 1720, was an important political leader in the colony of Maryland. Originally born in Ireland in 1685, Dulany immigrated to Maryland around 1703, as an indentured servant and became a lawyer. He served as a member of the Maryland Assembly for twenty years, beginning in 1722. Initially, Dulany led the legislative opposition to Charles Calvert and the proprietor's power, but after Calvert named him to higher colonial offices, Dulany supported Calvert. Dulany even became a member of the governor's council in 1742, and helped win passage of the Tobacco Inspection Act in 1747.

Calvert enlisted the help of Daniel Dulany. An immigrant from Ireland, Dulany had come to Maryland as an indentured servant, working as a clerk in his master's law practice. After his term was up, he became a successful lawyer. By the 1740s, he was one of Maryland's wealthiest landowners.

Traveling along the southern Potomac, Dulany found rich farmland and plenty of trees for building houses. He thought it was the perfect place for a settlement and in 1744 bought 20,000 acres (8,094 ha). To lure settlers to the area, Dulany offered farmers plots of 100 to 300 acres (40 to 121 ha) at a cheap price. He was especially successful at attracting German farmers and craftspeople, who were well known in the colonies for being hardworking. The population grew fast, especially at Frederick Town, which Dulany had named in 1745 after Charles Calvert's son. By 1750, Frederick Town was the largest town in the colony.

CHARLES WILLSON PEALE: MARYLAND ARTIST

Born in Queen Anne County, Maryland, in 1741, Charles Willson Peale was one of the most distinguished painters in colonial America. In the 1760s, he began painting portraits of prominent people and families in Maryland, Virginia, and Pennsylvania. After studying with Pennsylvania artist Benjamin West in London, he returned to Annapolis, where he became involved in the cause of American independence. During the American Revolution, he moved to Philadelphia. In addition to serving in the city's militia, Peale painted many of the delegates to the Continental Congress. His most famous subject was George Washington. The first to paint the future president's portrait, Peale produced about sixty works of Washington during the painter's lifetime.

The Athens of the Americas

But the most important town in colonial Maryland was still Annapolis. Since 1694, it had been the colony's capital. It also emerged as the center of Maryland's cultural life. In fact, Annapolis was nicknamed the "Athens of America," after the capital of ancient Greece, whose civilization was revered by educated eighteenth-century Americans.

Annapolis's reputation came in part from its beautiful architecture. While most Marylanders still lived in simple wooden structures, the wealthiest families in Annapolis built huge brick mansions. Many were two-story structures designed in the Georgian style, then popular in England. As their wealth grew, families often built additional wings onto the original building.

Craftspeople flocked to Annapolis, knowing the rich needed all sorts of wares to fill these mansions. The town was full of furniture makers, portrait painters, silversmiths, and clock makers.

Charles Willson Peale made this painting of Dr. Henry Stevenson's Georgian-style home (watercolor on ivory, around 1769). In 1769, Dr. Stevenson administered the first smallpox inoculation in a hospital in Baltimore. He called his estate Parnassus, in honor of the mountain in Greece that in Greek mythology was sacred to Apollo and the Muses. The Georgian style of architecture usually featured symmetrical structures that had two floors, central or end chimneys, a side gable roof, and classical details in decorations.

Annapolis was also the home of the *Maryland Gazette*, the first newspaper published in the Chesapeake region. It often printed humorous essays by members of the Tuesday Club, a group of Annapolis's best literary talents known for their wit.

For entertainment, the people of Annapolis frequented theaters and concerts. But the biggest social event of the year was the annual September horse race sponsored by the Jockey Club. Marylanders loved horse races. Even in farm communities, people gathered together to watch the area's fastest nags compete against one another. These rural races were rowdy affairs, accompanied by heavy drinking and gambling. The Jockey Club's races were much more genteel. They were run only by thoroughbreds, often imported from England. But both types of races served similar purposes. They were excuses for colonists to show off their prized possessions—symbols of a prosperity enjoyed, for a time, by Marylanders of all classes.

CHAPTER 6

Growing Discontent

In the late eighteenth century, Maryland continued to grow and thrive. But prosperity did little to quiet the simmering anger bubbling up among its people. Marylanders had long resisted rules set down by the proprietor. But as the century wore on, they came to resent the authority of the English king just as much. Jonathan Boucher, an official at the time, aptly summed up the feelings of unease and unrest sweeping through all of Maryland society: "[T]imes were grown beyond measure troublesome: men's minds were restless and dissatisfied, for ever discontented and grumbling at the present state of things, and for ever projecting reformations."

Fighting the Proprietor

The dissatisfactions with the proprietor, voiced most loudly by the members of the assembly's lower house, were nothing new. Marylanders had long been annoyed by the rents and fines the proprietor demanded. But they became increasingly irritated by the fees collected by sheriffs, judges, court clerks, and other officials appointed by the proprietor. These officials required a fee for just about every transaction they oversaw. (For instance, no witness could give testimony in court without first paying the judge a certain sum.) Such officials, usually the proprietor's friends, could make a fortune serving in these posts.

Assemblymen also tangled with the proprietor over which English laws applied to the people of Maryland. The proprietor believed he had the right to choose among the laws. The delegates, though, stubbornly insisted that they were entitled to all the rights of English citizens.

Tensions in the colony grew even more heated during the French and Indian War (1754–1763). This conflict pitted the British colonists and their Native American allies against French settlers and their Native American allies. The lower house was less than eager to help fund the war. Its members held that it was the proprietor's responsibility to protect the colony from enemies. After much debate, the assembly finally allocated money for the war. Much of it, though, came from a tax on landowners, including the proprietor himself. The king let Frederick Calvert, the sixth Lord Baltimore, know he was none too pleased by Maryland's lack of support.

Questioning the King

By the time of the war, Marylanders were just as irritated by the king as he was by them. One of their gripes was with the policy of transportation. (The word "transportation" here means banishment to a penal colony.) This policy, adopted by the English government in 1717, called for the banishing of English convicts to the American colonies. There they were bought and sold as indentured servants, usually for a term of seven years. Because English ships carrying the convicts often stopped off at the Chesapeake Bay, Maryland got more than its share of convicts. By 1767, about 10,000 English criminals were in Maryland.

Small farmers, who could not afford slaves, welcomed the convicts, as their labor was cheap. But few other Marylanders were happy to have these criminals in their midst. For decades, Maryland's politicians protested transportation, but the king largely ignored their complaints.

The *Maryland Gazette*'s headline for Thursday, October 10, 1765, announced that it was suspending publication. The *Gazette*'s owners decided to stop printing the newspaper because of the Stamp Act. The newspaper had to include a spot for the despised stamp on the front page, near the bottom right corner of the paper, pictured here at the right. The British parliament passed the Stamp Act to raise money in the colonies to help pay for maintaining British troops in America. Purchase of stamps was required for all legal papers, licenses, contracts, newspapers, pamphlets, and even playing cards.

Even more upsetting to Marylanders were the new taxes the king levied on the colonists after the war. Many Marylanders, both poor and rich, were suffering hard times in the 1760s. Tobacco prices dropped, making it impossible for many merchants and farmers to pay their debts. They were certainly not in the mood to funnel more of their income to the English king.

Popular Protests

One tax was called for in the Stamp Act of 1765. With this law, England required that all newspapers and legal documents in the colonies bear a stamp sold by the English government. Jonas Green, editor of the *Maryland Gazette*, feverishly attacked the act, vowing that he would shut the paper down before paying a penny of the tax. Average citizens showed their own displeasure through more violent means. One mob set fire to a dummy of the official charged with collecting the tax. Another set ablaze the building where the stamps were stored.

England repealed the Stamp Act the next year, replacing it in 1767 with the Townshend Acts. These acts placed taxes on all English goods entering America. Marylanders responded with a policy of nonimportation. Instead of importing English goods, they agreed to buy only American-made items. Maryland's merchants were particularly supportive of nonimportation, but not just for political reasons. The policy brought prices up for all sorts of necessities, which for merchants meant bigger and bigger profits.

Amid this political unrest, a new group of leaders emerged in the lower house. Loudly critical of the proprietor, they were known as the popular party. But anger toward governmental authority was increasingly found not only in the assembly house, but also throughout Maryland. One writer in the *Maryland Gazette* maintained that the minds of many ordinary colonists were "poisoned to such a Degree, that far from being ashamed of resisting subordinate Authority, they even glory in their audacious Insults of Government itself."

On an October night in 1774, Annapolis was the site of a dramatic display of their furor. A ship called the *Peggy Stewart*

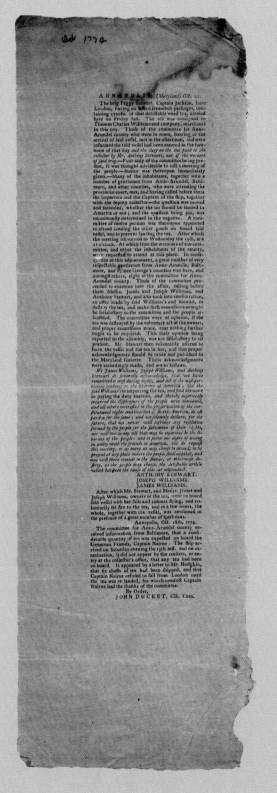

The Burning of the Peggy Stewart (top), painted by Francis Blackwell Mayer in 1896, illustrates the brigantine's demise in October 1774. Anthony Stewart, the ship's owner, had paid the controversial tea tax that was imposed by Parliament. By paying the tax, Stewart violated the nonimportation resolution that the colonists had enacted in protest. Angry colonists threatened to injure Stewart, or worse, burn his shipment of tea and the ship itself. An Annapolis broadside dated October 20, 1774 *(right)*, described the scene: "The brig *Peggy Stewart*, Captain from London having on board seventeen packages containing 2320 lb of that detestable weed tea arrived here on Friday . . ." For a partial transcription, see page 55.

arrived at its port. The ship's cargo included more than 2,000 pounds (907 kg) of English tea. The ship's owner, Anthony Stewart, had secretly paid the tax on the tea in violation of the nonimportation policy.

Stewart's secret was discovered. Maryland's leaders gathered to decide what to do. Some wanted to tar and feather Stewart and set fire to his ship. Others, though, pushed for a more moderate course of action. They said burning the tea would be enough. But this did not satisfy Stewart's angriest critics, who vowed to gather a crowd to dole out a harsher punishment. Fearing for his life, Stewart volunteered to make an additional sacrifice. In view of the entire city, he set his own ship on fire. As the *Peggy Stewart* burned, one thing was clear: Maryland was ready for a revolution.

CHAPTER 7

From Colony to State

In the fall of 1774, the people of Maryland were not the only colonists with revolutionary fever. While Marylanders cheered the torching of the *Peggy Stewart*, representatives of all thirteen English colonies gathered in Philadelphia for the first Continental Congress. At this meeting, the colonial leaders discussed the fate of America. They had to make a decision—whether or not to fight for independence from English control.

Instead of declaring war, the delegates opted to send a petition of grievances to the king. In November, the congressmen returned home and prepared to reconvene the following summer. But before the next congress, British troops and American militiamen exchanged gunfire in April 1775, in the Massachusetts towns of Lexington and Concord. The American Revolution had begun.

A Vote for Independence

News of the Massachusetts battles stirred up excitement in Marylanders ready to rebel. But not all Marylanders were enthusiastic about the war. Many were afraid all law and order would crumble as Maryland was taken over by angry mobs. Some worried that the chaos would inspire further rebellions of slaves, indentured servants, and convicts.

Others opposed the revolution because they did not want a change in government. Many were wealthy planters, merchants, and officeholders who had thrived under the proprietorship. But

Maryland-born artist Charles Willson Peale painted this portrait of William Paca *(left)* in 1772. Paca was born in Hartford County, Maryland, and went to London to study law. After his return to the colony, Paca was elected to the First and Second Continental Congresses. He signed the Declaration of Independence as one of Maryland's delegates. Paca later served as governor of the state from 1782 to 1785. Peale also painted Samuel Chase *(right)* around 1773. Chase, who was born in Princess Anne, Maryland, served as a member of the Continental Congress and signed the Declaration of Independence. President George Washington later appointed Chase to the U.S. Supreme Court.

the war was also unpopular with some of Maryland's poor. They saw that the colony's leaders were largely rich and powerful men who wanted to keep the English king out of their business. These poor Marylanders did not want to fight a war to protect the land and property of the wealthy.

On both sides, emotions were high. In Baltimore, armed battles broke out between those who supported the war and those who did not. At the same time, Maryland's leaders established a new government of elected officials that was to meet at a convention each year in Annapolis. Although they created the convention in complete defiance of the proprietor and the king, the delegates were divided about declaring Maryland's independence from England. In 1776, as Maryland's representatives were preparing for the summer's Continental Congress, the Annapolis convention delegates specifically instructed the representatives not to agree to a declaration of independence without first getting the Annapolis convention's consent.

The indecision of the Maryland representatives annoyed some of the more militant congressmen. Summing up their sentiment, Richard Henry Lee of Virginia angrily dismissed their behavior as "namby pamby." But by the middle of June, Maryland's leaders determined that there was no going back. With the convention's blessing, Maryland's congressmen signed the Declaration of Independence.

At least in the colonists' eyes, colonial Maryland no longer existed. Maryland was now a state. In September 1776, the state government created a constitution. For impoverished Marylanders, the new government was hardly better than the proprietor's rule. As in the past, only white men with property could vote, and only very wealthy property owners could run for governor. These restrictions ensured that power would remain firmly in the hands of the well-to-do.

At War

For the average Marylander, becoming a citizen of the new United States meant sacrifice. The American army needed food and other necessities. Each state was expected to round up a

This page from the Mordecai Gist Papers indicates the names of the soldiers from Maryland who reported for duty in January 1779, during the Revolutionary War. Supplies for Maryland troops were scarce, and there was a general lack of discipline among the soldiers. Some Maryland soldiers who were drafted to fight in the war ended up deserting.

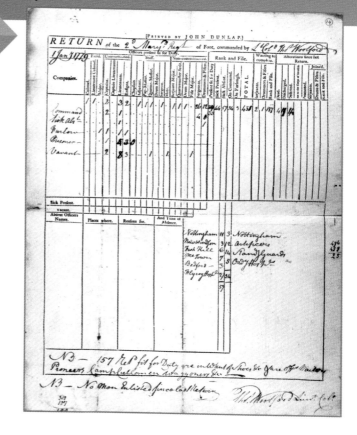

certain amount of supplies. Among the goods Maryland had to contribute were 20,000 barrels of flour and 56,000 bushels of corn. Individuals were asked to donate additional goods, such as blankets and shoes. And as troops traveled through Maryland, they often seized wagons, horses, wheat, and anything else they needed.

The greatest sacrifice, though, was made by men charged with fighting the war. Congress wanted Maryland to assemble eight regiments of soldiers. Recruiting enough men was difficult. At first, the state relied on volunteers, but later it instituted a draft. Wealthy men, however, could send a servant in their place.

Throughout the war, Maryland had a hard time obtaining provisions for its fighters. Often the soldiers did not have enough food. At times, especially at the beginning of the war, many did not even have guns. A lack of discipline among the troops was also a problem. Resenting the draft, some soldiers paid little heed to their officers' commands. Others simply deserted.

Even so, many soldiers from Maryland distinguished themselves. There were no major battles in Maryland, but Marylanders fought in colonies to the north and to the south. They earned high praise for their marksmanship, a talent probably honed through years of hunting. In 1776, after the Battle of Long Island, Tench Tilghman, a member of General George Washington's staff, wrote about the Marylanders that "no regular troops ever made a more gallant resistance."

Battles at Sea

But Maryland's greatest contribution to the war effort came from its shipyards and factories. Unlike other important cities such as New York and Philadelphia, Baltimore was not occupied by British troops. As a result, it became a manufacturing center, producing items that the colonists previously imported from England (such as wool, paper, and linen). The city's shipbuilding industry also provided many of the vessels needed to battle British ships.

Some Baltimore sailors joined the American navy. But many more were privateers. The American government authorized these commanders of privately owned ships to attack and loot British vessels. Attracted both by adventure and by the desire to serve their country, about 250 privateers operated out of Baltimore. They took hundreds of British ships, making off with ammunition, clothing, flour, and other badly needed supplies.

With the help of Maryland's soldiers and sailors, the American army won the revolution. On September 3, 1783, representatives of the U.S. Congress signed the peace treaty with the English. No

ARCHAEOLOGY OF COLONIAL MARYLAND

Much of what we know about colonial Maryland is found in historical records—documents, letters, and other writings the colonists left behind. But by systematically digging up sites where these colonists once lived, archaeologists have also contributed greatly to our knowledge of the first Marylanders. In 1990, archaeologists made a dramatic discovery at the site of the Brick Chapel, built in St. Mary's in the 1660s. They found three lead coffins that had been undisturbed for centuries. One coffin contained the bones of Philip Calvert, the youngest son of George Calvert, the first Lord Baltimore. In the other two were probably the bones of Philip Calvert's first wife, Anne, and a child, probably from his second marriage.

longer under English control, the colonial era truly came to an end throughout America.

Nearly five years later, seventy-four representatives from all over Maryland met in Annapolis. There, they voted on whether to ratify, or approve, the U.S. Constitution. On April 28, 1788, a large majority of sixty-three voted for ratification, and Maryland became the seventh state to officially join the United States of America. The next month, crowds marched through the streets of Baltimore to celebrate. The parade ended at a site now called Federal Hill, where the crowd enjoyed an enormous picnic and a fireworks display.

Celebrating Maryland's Past

In the years since the American Revolution, much has changed in Maryland. The population has grown from about 320,000 in 1790 to nearly 5,300,000 in 2000. Tobacco growing is no longer Maryland's central business. The state's economy now depends less

Archaeologists, pictured here in 1979, work hard to study the artifacts and structures they discovered along the banks of the St. Marys River at St. Mary's City. St. Mary's City is believed to be the first settlement in Maryland. Although the original city no longer stands, Historic St. Mary's City is an archaeological site that includes a reconstructed statehouse, a working colonial farm, a replica of the square-rigged *Dove*, and reconstructions of several other public buildings.

on agriculture and more on the financial and service industries. Baltimore remains Maryland's largest city and a major American port, although it is no longer the thriving manufacturing center it once was.

Despite the passage of centuries, one thing has not changed: Marylanders' fascination with the region's colonial history. Each year, on March 25, thousands celebrate Maryland Day. The state holiday commemorates the day in 1634 when the *Ark* and the *Dove* arrived at St. Clement's Island, bringing the first colonists to the region. Before that day, Maryland was just a dream of the proprietor. But after that day, it became a home for many, a refuge for some, and a prison for others—all made real through the blood and sweat of the earliest Marylanders.

TIMELINE

1632 — Charles I of England grants Maryland to Cecilius Calvert.

March 25, 1634 — About 150 English settlers land on St. Clement's Island in the Chesapeake Bay.

1635 — Maryland's first assembly meets in St. Mary's City.

April 21, 1649 — The Maryland Assembly passes An Act Concerning Religion.

1652 — Maryland negotiates a peace treaty with the Susquehannock.

1654 — Protestant rebels defeat the proprietor's army at the Battle of the Severn.

1666 — George Alsop publishes *A Character of the Province of Maryland*.

1689 — The Protestant Association rebels against officials of the Maryland proprietorship.

1692 — The Maryland Assembly makes the Church of England (Anglican Church) the official religion of the colony.

1694 — Anne Arundell Town (later renamed Annapolis) becomes the capital of Maryland.

1715 — The English crown restores the Maryland proprietorship, placing the colony again under the control of the Calvert family.

1717 — England begins transporting convicts to Maryland and the other American colonies.

1765 — Marylanders protest the Stamp Act.

1775–1783 — Soldiers from Maryland fight for independence from England during the American Revolution.

1776 — Delegates from Maryland sign the Declaration of Independence. Maryland leaders draft Maryland's first state constitution.

1788 — Maryland ratifies the U.S. Constitution and becomes the seventh U.S. state.

PRIMARY SOURCE TRANSCRIPTIONS

Page 9: Excerpt from the Charter of Maryland, Granted by Charles I to Lord Baltimore, June 1632

Transcription

Charles, by the Grace of God, of England, Scotland, France, and Ireland, king, Defender of the Faith, &c. To all to whom these Presents come, Greeting.

II. Whereas our well beloved and right trusty Subject Caecilius Calvert, Baron of Baltimore, in our Kingdom of Ireland, Son and Heir of George Calvert, Knight, late Baron of Baltimore, in our said Kingdom of Ireland, treading in the steps of his Father, being animated with a laudable, and pious Zeal for extending the Christian Religion, and also the Territories of our Empire, hath humbly besought Leave of us, that he may transport, by his own Industry, and Expense, a numerous Colony of the English Nation, to a certain Region, herein after described, in a Country hitherto uncultivated, in the Parts of America . . .

We . . . do Give, Grant and Confirm, unto the aforesaid Caecilius, now Baron of Baltimore, his Heirs, and Assigns, all that Part of the Peninsula . . . lying in the Parts of America, between the Ocean on the East and the Bay of Chesapeake on the West, divided from the Residue thereof by a Right Line drawn from the Promontory . . . called Watkin's Point . . . near the river Wigloo, on the West, unto the main Ocean on the East; and between that Boundary on the South, unto that Part of the Bay of Delaware on the North, which lieth under the Fortieth Degree of North Latitude from the Equinoctial . . . And all that Tract of Land . . . passing from the . . . Delaware Bay, in a right Line, by the Degree aforesaid, unto the true meridian of the first Fountain of the River of Pattowmack, thence verging toward the South, unto the further Bank of the said River, and following the same on the West and South, unto a certain Place, called Cinquack, situate near the mouth of the said River, where it disembogues into the aforesaid Bay of Chesapeake, and thence by the shortest Line unto the aforesaid Promontory or Place, called Watkin's Point; so that the whole tract of land, divided by the Line aforesaid, between the main Ocean and Watkin's Point, unto the Promontory called Cape Charles, and every the Appendages thereof, may entirely remain excepted for ever to Us, our Heirs and Successors.

Page 19: Excerpt from An Act Concerning Religion (1649)

Transcription

An Act Concerning Religion
. . . Be it therefore Ordered and Enacted by the right honorable Cecilius Lord Baron of Baltimore absolute Lord and Proprietary of this Province with the advice and Consent of the General Assembly that whatsoever Person or Persons within this province and

the Islands thereto Belonging shall from henceforth Blaspheme God that is Curse him or deny our Saviour Jesus Christ to be the Son of God or shall deny the holy Trinity the Father Son & Holy Ghost on the Godhead of any of the said three Persons of the Trinity or the unity of the Godhead or shall use or utter any reproachful speeches words or Language Concerning the said holy Trinity or any of the said three Persons thereof shall be punished with death & Confiscation or forfeiture of all his or her lands and Goods to the Lord Proprietary and his heirs . . . and be it also Enacted by the Authority . . . that no Person or Persons whatsoever within this Province . . . [professing] to believe in Jesus Christ shall from henceforth be in any ways troubled molested or discountenanced for or in respect of his or her Religion nor in the free exercise thereof within this Province . . . nor any way Compelled to the Belief for exercise of any other Religion against his or her consent so as they be not unfaithful to the Lord Proprietary or molest or Conspire against the Civil Government established or to be established in this Province under him or his heirs . . . and that all and every Person and persons that shall presume Contrary to this Act and the true intent and meaning thereof directly or indirectly either in Person or estate willfully to wrong disturb trouble or molest any Person whatsoever within this province professing to Believe in Jesus Christ for or in respect of his or her Religion or the free Exercise thereof with this Province other than is provided for in the Act that such Person or persons so offending shall be compelled to pay treble damages to the party so wronged or molested and for every such Offence shall forfeit 20s Sterling in money or the Value thereof . . . half thereof for the use of the Lord Proprietary and his heirs . . . and the other half for the use of the Party so wronged or molested as aforesaid and if the Party so Offending as aforesaid shall Refuse or be unable to recompence the Party so Grieved or to satisfy such fine or forfeiture then such offender shall be severely [punished] by publick whipping and imprisonment . . .

Page 25: Excerpt from An Act for Erecting a County Court

Transcription

Be it Enacted By the Lord Proprietarie of this Province by and with the advice and approbation of the Freemen of the same that all causes of appeal from inferiour Courts and all causes whatsoever civill determinable in any Court of common Law in England and all causes for recovery of Legacy's and all Causes matrimonial (forasmuch as concerns the triall of Covenants and Contracts and the punishment of faults committed against the same) . . . and all Crimes and offences whatsoever) not extending to felony or treason by the Laws of this Province) for which any certain punishment is appointed by the laws of this Province or by the Common Law of England shall be heard and determined finally by and before the chief Justice of the Province for the time being . . .

Which said chief Justice shall or may appoint a Register for the Recording of all matters pertaining to that office . . . and the said Register shall be a Court of Record and shall be called the County Court...

Page 42: Excerpt from a broadside, Annapolis, Maryland, October 20, 1774.

Transcription
ANNAPOLIS (Maryland) Oct. 20.

The brig Peggy Stewart, Captain Jackson, from London, having on board seventeen packages, containing 2320lb. of that detestable weed tea, arrived here on Friday last. The tea was consigned to Thomas Charles Williams and company, merchants in this city. Those of the committee for Anne-Arundel county who were in town, hearing of the arrival of said vessel, met in the afternoon, and were informed the said vessel had been entered in the forenoon of that day and the duty on the tea paid to the collector by Mr. Anthony Stewart, one of the owners of said brig.— . . . Many of the inhabitants . . . met, and having called before them the importers and the Captain of the ship, together with the deputy collector—the question was moved and seconded, whether the tea should be landed in America or not; and the question being put, was unanimously determined in the negative. A committee of twelve persons was thereupon appointed to attend landing the other goods on board said vessel, and to prevent landing the tea . . . The committee were of opinion, if the tea was destroyed by the voluntary act of the owners, and proper concessions made, that nothing further ought to be required . . . Mr. Stewart then voluntarily offered to burn the vessel and the tea in her, and that proper acknowledgments should be made and published in the Maryland Gazette. Those acknowledgments were accordingly made, and are as follows.

We James Williams, Joseph Williams, and Anthony Stewart do severally acknowledge, that we have committed a most daring insult, and act of the most pernicious tendency to the liberties of America; we the said Williams's in importing the tea, and said Stewart in paying the duty thereon, and thereby deservedly incurred the displeasure of the people now convened, and all others interested in the preservation of the constitutional rights and liberties of North-America, do ask pardon for the same; and we solemnly declare, for the future, that we never will infringe any resolution formed by the people for the salvation of their rights, nor will we do any act that may be injurious to the liberties of the people: and to shew our desire of living in amity with the friends to America, we do request this meeting, or as many as may choose to attend, to be present at any place where the people shall appoint, and we will there commit to the flames, or otherwise destroy, as the people may choose, the detestable article which has been the cause of this our misconduct . . .

GLOSSARY

assembly The law-making body of a colony or a state, made up of elected representatives and appointed councilmen.

banish To force to leave an area.

charter A document from a king or other sovereign power that grants certain rights to a person or group.

colony An area under the political control of a parent country.

epidemic An outbreak of a disease.

Georgian style A style of architecture that was developed in England and that became popular in the American colonies. Named after the English kings George I, George II, George III, and George IV, the style was popular from about 1714 to 1820 and was influenced by the monumental architecture of ancient Greece and Rome and from the Renaissance and Baroque periods. Georgian buildings usually are symmetrical in design and are decorated with elements such as pediments, pilasters, and egg and dart moldings.

heir A person who inherits a title, a rank, or an estate.

indentured servant A person who agrees to work in the service of another person for a specific length of time, especially in return for payment of travel expenses.

land grant An area of land given to a person by a government.

manor A tract of land in which the owner has control over both the land and the people living on it.

militia An army of citizens who are not professional soldiers.

nag A racehorse.

persecute To mistreat or punish a person or a group of people because of their religion, race, or beliefs.

privateer A commander of a privately owned vessel authorized by a government to attack enemy ships during wartime.

proprietor A person who owns an area of land or a business.

Puritan A member of a group of English Protestants who, in the sixteenth and seventeenth centuries, promoted religious discipline and the simplification of the rituals of the Church of England.

ratified Approved; agreed to officially.

tolerance The practice of respecting others' beliefs.

transportation An English policy of the eighteenth century that called for relocating criminals to the American colonies.

FOR MORE INFORMATION

Historic London Town & Gardens
839 Londontown Road
Edgewater, MD 21037
(410) 222-1919
Web site: http://www.historiclondontown.com

Historic St. Mary's City
Route 5
St. Mary's City, MD 20686
(301) 862-0960
Web site: http://www.stmaryscity.org

Maryland Historical Society
201 West Monument Street
Baltimore, MD 21201
(410) 685-3750
Web site: http://www.mdhs.org

Maryland State Archives
350 Rowe Boulevard
Annapolis, MD 21401
(410) 260-6400
Web site: http://www.mdarchives.state.md.us

Sotterley Plantation
Route 245
Hollywood, MD 20636
(301) 373-2280
Web site: http://www.sotterley.com

St. Clement's Island–Potomac River Museum
38370 Point Breeze Road
Colton's Point, MD 20626
(301) 769-2222
Web site: http://www.co.saint-marys.md.us/recreate/museums/
   stclementsisland.asp

Web Sites

Due to the changing nature of Internet links, the Rosen Publishing
Group, Inc., has developed an online list of Web sites related to the
subject of this book. This site is updated regularly. Please use this link
to access the list:

http://www.rosenlinks.com/pstc/mary

FOR FURTHER READING

Fradin, Dennis Brindell. *The Maryland Colony* (The Thirteen
    Colonies). Chicago, IL: Children's Press, 1990.
Jensen, Ann. *Leonard Calvert and the Maryland Adventure*.
    Centreville, MD: Tidewater Publishers, 1998.
Kent, Deborah. *In the Middle Colonies* (How We Lived . . .). New
    York, NY: Benchmark Books, 1999.
Lough, Loree. *Lord Baltimore: English Politician and Colonist*.
    Philadelphia, PA: Chelsea House Publishers, 2000.
Streissguth, Thomas. *Maryland*. San Diego, CA: Lucent Books, 2001.

BIBLIOGRAPHY

Alsop, George. *Alsop's Maryland: A Character of the Province of Maryland.* Bowie, MD: Heritage Books, 2001.

Arnett, Eric, Robert J. Brugger, and Edward C. Papenfuse. *Maryland: A New Guide to the Old Line State*. 2nd ed. Baltimore, MD: Johns Hopkins University Press, 1999.

Brugger, Robert J. *Maryland: A Middle Temperament, 1634–1980*. Baltimore, MD: Johns Hopkins University Press, 1988.

Land, Aubrey C. *Colonial Maryland: A History*. Millwood, NY: KTO Press, 1981.

Main, Gloria L. *Tobacco Colony: Life in Early Maryland, 1650–1720*. Princeton, NJ: Princeton University Press, 1982.

Tate, Thad W., and David L. Ammerman, eds. *The Chesapeake in the Seventeenth Century: Essays on Anglo-American Society*. New York, NY: W. W. Norton, 1979.

PRIMARY SOURCE IMAGE LIST

Page 1: A view of the port of Baltimore, 1752. Taken from John Moale's sketch of 1752. At the left, near the single-masted sloop is the tobacco inspection warehouse on Charles Street. At the top of the hill, near the center of the illustration, is Old St. Paul's Church.

Page 8: *George Calvert*, a portrait painted around 1881 by John Alfred Vintner (1828-1905). Vintner's oil painting was based on an original painting from around 1625 by Daniel Mytens the Elder and is housed in the collection of the Maryland State Archives, Annapolis, Maryland.

Page 9: Charter of Maryland, granted to George Calvert, Lord Baltimore, by King Charles I on June 20, 1632. Maryland State Archives.

Page 11: *Nova Terrae-Mariae tabula*, a 1671 map of Maryland and parts of Virginia based on an engraved map of 1635, published by John Ogilby in his atlas, entitled *America* (London, 1671).

Page 12: Colored engraving of The Tovvne of Secota by Thedor de Bry, 1590, based on a 1585 watercolor by John White. De Bry's print was published in *America* (1590), pt. 1, pl. XXX. Housed in the New York Public Library.

Page 19 (left): An Act Concerning Religion, passed by the general assembly, upper house, on April 21, 1649. Original document housed in the Maryland State Archives, Annapolis.

Page 19 (right): Rosary beads, found at the site of St. Mary's City, the first settlement in Maryland.

Page 21: *A Land-Skip of the Province of Mary Land*, 1666 map that originally appeared in George Alsop's *A Character of the Province of Maryland*. This particular map was reprinted in Gowan's *Biblioteca Americana*, Volume 1, in New York in 1869, now housed in the Maryland State Archives, Annapolis.

Page 22: Title page of George Alsop's *A Character of the Province of Maryland*, published by Peter Dring in London in 1666.

Page 25: "An Act for the Erecting of a County Court," *Proceedings and Acts of the General Assembly of Maryland, January 1637/8-September 1664*. Housed in the Maryland State Archives, Annapolis.

Page 26: *The Hanging Judge*, engraved by Charles Grignion (1717-1810).

Page 29: An engraving of the Charles County courthouse and ordinary, 1697, housed in the Maryland State Archives, Annapolis.

Page 31: Map cartouche from *A Map of the Most Inhabited Part of Virginia Containing the Whole Province of Maryland with Part of Pensilvania, New Jersey and North Carolina*, drawn by Joshua Fry and Peter Jefferson, 1775. Private collection.

Page 33: *Grey's Inn Creek Shipyard*, an oil painting on panel by an anonymous artist, from around 1750, housed by the Maryland Historical Society.

Page 35: *Daniel Dulaney the Elder*, a portrait painted around 1720 by an anonymous artist, is housed by the Maryland Historical Society.

Page 37: Charles Willson Peale (1741-1827) painted *Full View of Parnassus, Home of Dr. Henry Stevenson* in watercolors on ivory around 1769. Housed in the Maryland Historical Society.

Page 40: The *Maryland Gazette*, front page, Thursday, October 10, 1765. Published in Baltimore. Housed in the Maryland State Archives.

Page 42 (left): Francis Blackwell Mayer's painting, entitled *The Burning of the Peggy Stewart*, oil on canvas, painted in 1896. Housed in the Maryland State Archives. Maryland Commission on Artistic Property.

Page 42 (right): A broadside printed by Anne Catharine Green, October 20, 1774, that relates the story of the burning of the *Peggy Stewart*. Housed in the Library of Congress.

Page 45 (left): A portrait of William Paca painted by Charles Willson Peale in 1772. Oil on mattress ticking. Housed in the Maryland Historical Society.

Page 45 (right): A portrait of Samuel Chase, painted in oil on canvas by Charles Willson Peale around 1773. Housed in the Maryland Historical Society.

Page 47: *Revolutionary War Troops Return for the Maryland Line*, January 1, 1779, housed in the Maryland Historical Society.

INDEX

About the Author

Liz Sonneborn is a writer living in Brooklyn, New York. A graduate of Swarthmore College, she has written more than fifty books for children and adults. Specializing in American history, she has a particular interest in the colonial and revolutionary war eras. Her books include *Benedict Arnold, John Paul Jones, The War of 1812,* and *The American West.*

Photo Credits

Cover, title page, pp. 5, 33, 35, 37, 45, 47 Courtesy of the Maryland Historical Society; pp. 8, 9, 15, 42 Courtesy of the Maryland Commission on Artistic Property of the Maryland State Archives [p. 8: John Alfred Vintner (1828-1905), George Calvert (1578/79-1632), date: c. 1881, medium: oil on canvas, dimensions: 62" x 42", accession number: MSA SC 1545-1101; p. 15: Florence Mackubin (1861-1918), Leonard Calvert (1606-1647), date: 1914, medium: oil on canvas, accession number: 1545-1106; p. 42: Francis Blackwell Mayer (1827-1899), *The Burning of the Peggy Stewart*, date: 1896, medium: oil on canvas, dimensions: 72" x 53", accession number: MSA SC 1545-1111]; pp. 11, 19, 21, 25, 29, 40 Courtesy of the Maryland State Archives [p. 11: Special Collections (Huntingfield Map Collection), Thomas Cecill (Engraver), *Nova Terrae-Mariae tabula*, 1635, MSA SC 1399-1-526; p. 19: General Assembly Upper House (Proceedings) MSA S977, dates: 1637-1658, description: MC accession number: 3860, MSA No.: S977-1, location: 2/20/4/42, pages 354-359; p. 21: Special Collections (Huntingfield Map Collection), George Alsop, *A Land-Skip of the Province of Mary Land*, 1666, MSA SC 1399-1-866; p. 25: General Assembly (Law Record) MSA S973, dates: 1638-1678, description: C & WH. February 1638/9-October 1678, partially transcribed in volume 1 of the Archives of Maryland series, accession number: 4535 MSA No.: S973-1, location: 2/19/2/1, pages 11-14; p. 29: Special Collections (Charles County Courthouse Collection), Courthouse at Moore's Lodge, from Charles County Court (Proceedings), *Liber V*, no. 1, 1697, MSA SC 1497-1-1; p. 40: Special Collections (Maryland State Law Library Collection of the *Maryland Gazette*), October 10, 1765, MSA SC 2311-1-6, the National Archives of the UK (PRO), ref. PSO 5/6]; p. 12, The New York Public Library/Art Resouce, N.Y., p. 17 © North Wind Picture Archives; pp. 19 (right), 50 © Lowell Georgia/Corbis; pp. 22, 26 © Getty Images; pp. 31 Library of Congress Geography and Map Division; p. 42 (right) Library of Congress Rare Book and Special Collections Division.

Editor: Kathy Kuhtz Campbell; Photo Researcher: Fernanda Rocha